Art and Culture

Exploring Mexican Artifacts

Measurement

Elisa Jordan, M.A.

Consultants

Lisa Ellick, M.A.
Math Specialist
Norfolk Public Schools

Pamela Estrada, M.S.Ed.
Teacher
Westminster School District

Publishing Credits

Rachelle Cracchiolo, M.S.Ed., *Publisher*
Conni Medina, M.A.Ed., *Managing Editor*
Dona Herweck Rice, *Series Developer*
Emily R. Smith, M.A.Ed., *Series Developer*
Diana Kenney, M.A.Ed., NBCT, *Content Director*
Stacy Monsman, M.A., *Editor*
Kristy Stark, M.A.Ed., *Editor*
Kevin Panter, *Graphic Designer*

Image Credits: p.9 (left) David Hilbert/Alamy Stock Photo; p.9 (right) OMAR TORRES/AFP/Getty Images; p.12 Danita Delimont/Alamy Stock Photo; p.16, Granger; p.17 (top) Romana Lilic/Getty Images; p.17 (bottom) Roberto Gennaro/iStock; p.18 De Agostini/G. Dagli Orti/Getty Images; p.21 (top) Burstein Collection / Getty Images; p.24 Werner Forman/Universal Images Group/Getty Images; p.25 Gerardo C. Lerner/Shutterstock.com; p.26 Herman Agopian/Getty Images

Teacher Created Materials
5301 Oceanus Drive
Huntington Beach, CA 92649-1030
http://www.tcmpub.com

ISBN 978-1-4258-5811-7

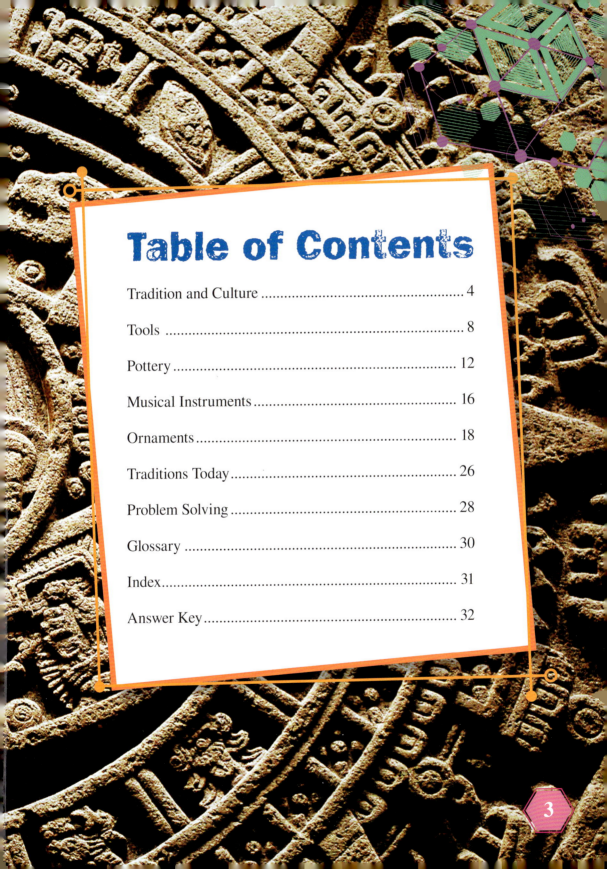

Table of Contents

Tradition and Culture

Mexico is a country with a strong sense of **tradition** and **culture**. The nation's history dates back prior to the arrival of Christopher Columbus in the Americas. The Olmec people were the first to live in Mexico. They lived near the Gulf of Mexico in the region that now makes up the states of Veracruz and Tabasco. The Olmec people can be traced back about 2,500 years. They are remembered for the giant head **sculptures** they carved out of stone.

The Zapotec, Maya, Aztec, and Toltec were other early cultures in the country. In some ways, the people lived a lot like people today. They had large cities. They used writing systems and calendars. They built temples and schools. They had systems for farming and government.

Things changed after Columbus arrived in the Americas in 1492. Europeans wanted to explore the land. Hernán Cortés, a Spanish explorer, sailed from Spain nearly 30 years after Columbus. After Cortés, more people came from Spain.

Cultures continued to mix in this region. Spanish culture started to influence the culture in Mexico. While some of the old buildings remained, Spaniards began to build new structures. They also introduced different ways of making tools, clothing, and food. They taught people to speak Spanish, too.

Olmec giant head

Maya fortress in Tulum, Mexico

Tourists explore a Maya step pyramid that was built for holding rituals.

This Maya warrior vase is thought to be from around AD 600–1000.

The Olmec, Zapotec, Maya, Aztec, and Toltec people left behind many **artifacts** that have helped people learn about their lives. Artifacts are objects made by humans. They give clues about the past. They may include buildings, tools, sculptures, **pottery**, and clothing. Artifacts help us understand how people cooked meals and where they lived. Some objects give information about how governments worked. Other objects tell about the things people liked to do for fun.

Artifacts link us to past cultures and people. This is important for many reasons. We can learn that we are not much different from our **ancestors**. They did many of the same things we do today. We can also learn that the way they did things can affect how we do things now. Many of these traditions have been handed down over the years. Understanding how a tradition began helps to keep traditions alive.

Mexico's past has shaped the present. The Spaniards arrived in Mexico in the 1500s. They brought and spread the Spanish language throughout the region. Today, people in Mexico still speak Spanish. People also use many of the same tools that were used back then.

The Toltec warriors standing in the city of Tyla are a symbol of battle.

Tools

Humans have been using tools for millions of years. Tools are objects that can help people do things like eat, cook, build, or make music. People in ancient Mexico used many tools that are still part of the culture today.

Metate

During **pre-Columbian** times, stone tools called *metates* (meh-TAH-tays) were used to grind plants, seeds, corn, and nuts.

Metates are made of two individual pieces. The large piece is called a grinding stone. This rectangular slab, with a slight incline on one end, is where food is placed. The grinding stone usually starts as a flat surface, but, over time, the flat surface becomes bowl-shaped. The smaller stone is called a *mano* (MAH-noh). *Mano* is the Spanish word for *hand*. The mano is moved by hand, in a back and forth motion, over the food on the grinding stone. This tool was an important part of daily life. Women woke early to make food for their families. They would most likely have spent a great deal of time kneeling over a metate grinding corn.

People still use metates today. Most modern metates have three short legs to keep the tools stable during the grinding process. Metates are used to make homemade tortillas, chocolate, and fresh salsa.

A woman finishes grinding corn with a metate.

metates

Metates are made in different sizes. Small metates are used to grind spices, medium metates are used to grind corn, and large metates are used to grind chocolate and coffee. Match each measurement to the metate it describes and answer the following question: are the metates longer than they are wide or wider than they are long? Explain how you know.

Lengths: $1\frac{1}{2}$ feet; 10 inches; 1 foot, 10 inches

Widths: $16\frac{1}{2}$ inches; 8 inches; 1 foot

Size of Metate	Length	Width
small		
medium		
large		

Molcajete

Molcajetes (MOHL-cah-heh-tays) are three-legged bowls. They date back thousands of years. Many ancient people used them, including the Maya and Aztecs. In fact, the molcajete is one of the world's oldest kitchen tools! Like metates, they are used to grind foods. Both tools are still used to make salsa and guacamole.

A molcajete has two pieces. It has a large stone bowl and a handheld grinding stone. The grinding stone is called a *tejolote* (TAY-ho-loh-tay). The tejolote is used to pound food in the bowl. The three legs keep it stable while food is ground.

Ancient Aztec and Maya molcajetes were carved out of **basalt**. This volcanic rock was soft enough to shape and carve. Craftsmen, or skilled workers, used the pecking method to repeatedly "peck" at the basalt stone. This motion eventually shaped the stones into bowls. Some artists formed the bowls into animal shapes, such as pigs and bulls.

Modern molcajetes are made from many kinds of stone including basalt. Molcajetes are still popular in homes and restaurants. Molcajetes can be used as serving dishes because their stone surfaces stay warm for a long time. That feature makes them perfect for using at parties!

molcajete

A molcajete must be seasoned, or prepared, before it is ready to use. This process has several steps requiring different amounts of time:

Step 1: Soak in water for 12 hours.

Step 2: Dry for 2 days.

Step 3: Grind rice with water and dry for $\frac{1}{2}$ day.

Step 4: Grind blend of spices, let set, and dry for 14 hours.

1. How many total hours does it take to season a molcajete?

2. How many minutes does it take?

3. Does this process take 3 or 4 days? Explain your reasoning.

A person grinds dried corn in a molcajete.

Pottery

In the past, people used **gourds** as **vessels** to carry water and other liquids. When pre-Columbian people began to make pottery, they used a similar gourd-like shape. Eventually, they started making other shapes, too.

Coil Method

People used the coil method to make pots. For this method, people rolled clay into long pieces. Then, they pinched the clay coils. Families often made simple pots that were small. Craftsmen made bigger and more detailed pots.

Once the pots were formed, they were placed on an open fire or in a fire pit. The fire hardened the clay, so the pots became strong enough to use for cooking, eating, and in ceremonies.

An artist smooths a bowl made with the coil method.

The pots were useful for daily activities but were also works of art. People used minerals to make paints. They painted pots with designs and shapes. They painted animals and people. They also pressed objects into the clay to make designs. The objects **imprinted** both sides of a pot.

People in each region of Mexico made their own styles of pottery. The different styles have helped historians determine where the pottery was made.

This pottery from northern Mexico was made by a potter named Juan Quezada Celado.

LET'S EXPLORE MATH

Javier drinks water out of his clay mug 3 times a day. The mug holds 350 milliliters of liquid. Did Javier drink more than or less than 1 liter of water? Remember, 1,000 milliliters = 1 liter.

Spanish Tools and Methods

Spanish settlers arrived in Mexico during the 1500s. They brought tools that helped make pottery. They shared their tools and techniques with the people of Mexico.

The Spaniards used **potter's wheels**. A potter's wheel is a machine that helps shape pottery into a round form. This tool made it easier to make pottery.

Spanish settlers also brought **kilns** to Mexico. A kiln is like an oven. Because it is enclosed, heat is more evenly distributed than an open fire. It's also easier to control the temperature. After a clay pot is formed, it is placed in a kiln to dry.

The Spanish people brought **glazes**, too. Glazes, which are similar to paint, were used to add color and designs to the pottery after it dried in the kiln.

The temperature rises in a fiery kiln.

Mexico quickly became part of a trade route after the Spanish settlers arrived. Ships sailed between countries and traded goods. These ships brought items from all over the world through Mexico. Mexico was between Spain and China on the trade route. Soon, pottery designs and colors started to reflect all three cultures.

Pottery is still popular in Mexico. Today's Mexican pottery styles are a mixture of the pre-Columbian and Spanish cultures.

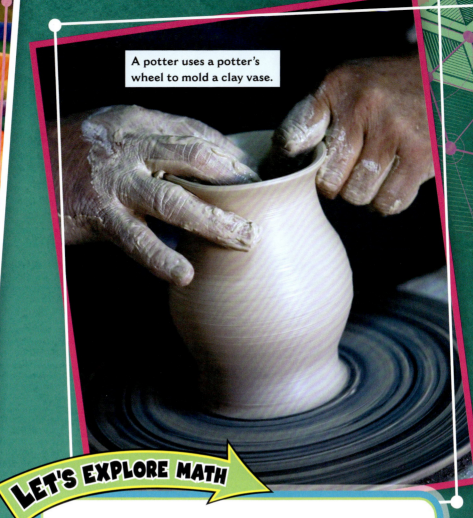

A potter uses a potter's wheel to mold a clay vase.

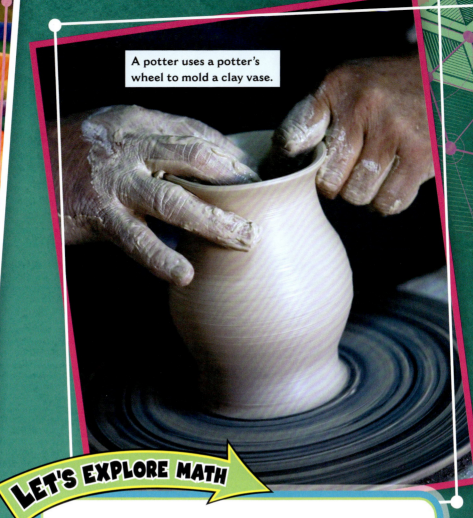

LET'S EXPLORE MATH

Karina makes her own pottery. She measures the height of each of her objects before she puts them into the kiln to make sure they'll fit.

Pottery Heights

16 inches	$6\frac{1}{2}$ inches	$14\frac{1}{8}$ inches
$5\frac{7}{8}$ inches	11 inches	$18\frac{1}{2}$ inches

1. What is the total height of all the pottery?

2. If Karina wants to redistribute the clay equally so that each object is the same height, how tall will each object be?

Musical Instruments

Music has always been an important part of Mexican culture. The Aztec, Maya, and Tarascan people all loved music. They made and performed music for over 2,000 years. Music was played to communicate with relatives and spirits. It was also used in celebration and in battle settings. At a young age, children learned to play instruments. Adults taught them many types of songs. They sang songs about good deeds, great leaders, and religion. These songs were used to celebrate special events. They also sang songs about having fun, love, and daily life.

Musical instruments were an important part of the songs. Aztec, Maya, and Tarascan people made and played a few different types of drums. Ayotl (I-oht) were drums made from turtle shells. Hollow logs were used to make Teponaztli (tehp-oh-NAHS-tlee) drums. Huehuetl (OOEH-ooeht) were drums made from wood with animal skin stretched across the top.

This drawing from about 1540 by a Spanish missionary shows his perception of Aztecs and their love of music.

A rattle was another type of musical instrument. Rattles were originally made by filling gourds with pebbles or beads. *Maracas* are the modern version of the rattle.

People in these ancient cultures also made trumpets from large shells called conches. Conches were blown to announce visitors to the area. They were used to track time. They were also used to signal the start of battle.

Drums, maracas, and conches are still important parts of Mexican culture. The people of Mexico continue to celebrate life with music.

A man blows a conch shell to honor an ancient cultural site in Mexico.

LET'S EXPLORE MATH

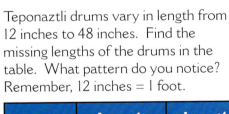

Teponaztli drums vary in length from 12 inches to 48 inches. Find the missing lengths of the drums in the table. What pattern do you notice? Remember, 12 inches = 1 foot.

Drum	Length (inches)	Length (feet)
A		$1\frac{1}{2}$
B		2
C		$2\frac{1}{2}$
D		3
E		$3\frac{1}{2}$

Ornaments

Ornaments are objects that are used to decorate things. People decorate homes, offices, and clothing with ornaments. Jewelry is a type of ornament that people wear. Early Mexican cultures made ornaments.

Statues, Sculptures, and Buildings

Statues are one type of ornament and are carved to reveal the **values** of a certain culture. In early Mexican culture, stones were carved to look like animals, people, plants, and gods.

The Olmec people carved statues that looked like huge heads. Experts think that these heads might have been modeled after people who were very important to them. The Olmec culture dates back before the Aztec or Maya cultures. So, these statues are some of the oldest in the world.

Stone was not the only material used to carve figures. People used pearls, shells, and amethyst gemstones. They used crystal, obsidian, and jade rocks, too. In China and Spain, jade was a highly valued stone because of its beauty. Jade was also valuable because many people believed it had healing powers. These cultures introduced jade to Mexico through trade routes.

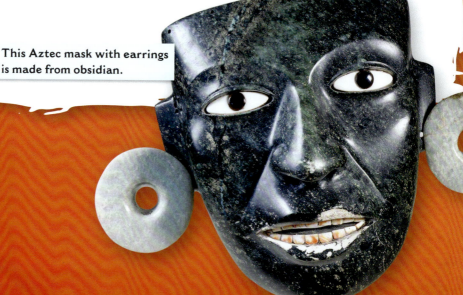

This Aztec mask with earrings is made from obsidian.

18

Olmec head

The Olmec Colossal Heads are a collection of at least 17 huge basalt sculptures. All of them vary in height. Find the missing heights of the statues in the table. Remember, 10 millimeters = 1 centimeter.

Statue	Height (millimeters)	Height (centimeters)
Tres Zapotes, Monument A		147
San Lorenzo, Head 10		180
La Venta, Monument 3	1,980	
San Lorenzo, Head 7	2,700	
Rancho La Cobata, Monument 1		340

Toltec warrior statues stand guard.

The people of western Mexico made many statues of people. They had a lot of respect for their ancestors. They made statues that showed the importance of families. They made **ceramic** sculptures of important family members when they died.

They also made statues of male and female couples. These are called marriage statues. Experts believe that these statues show the ancestors who started a specific family line. These statues reminded people about their family history.

The people of this region made statues that showed other things, too. They made warriors and dancers. They made statues of musicians and people playing ball. They made statues that reflected their rituals. These statues show what daily life was like.

These figures from a Mexican tomb are painted with special designs.

When Spaniards came to the region, they brought items that reflected their own culture. They brought statues. They built many new churches in the region, too. They decorated these buildings with statues that were important to their religion.

After a while, the pre-Columbian and Spanish cultures mixed together to form a new culture. People made things that showed this new culture. For instance, Mexico had more colorful clay than what was found in Spain. So, pottery and statues became more colorful.

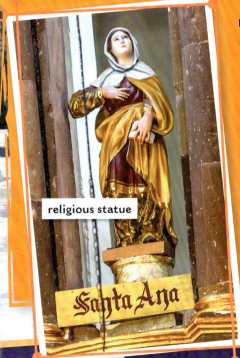

religious statue

Santa Ana

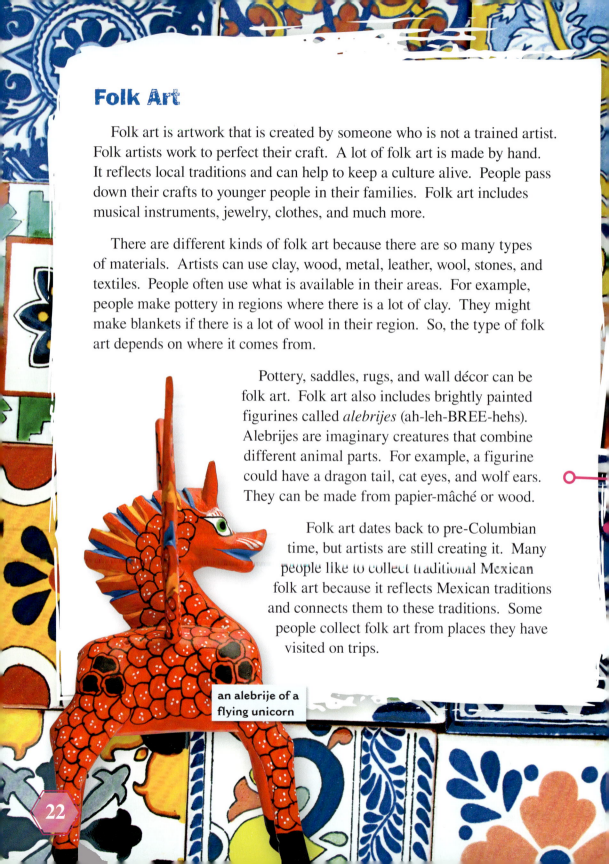

Folk Art

Folk art is artwork that is created by someone who is not a trained artist. Folk artists work to perfect their craft. A lot of folk art is made by hand. It reflects local traditions and can help to keep a culture alive. People pass down their crafts to younger people in their families. Folk art includes musical instruments, jewelry, clothes, and much more.

There are different kinds of folk art because there are so many types of materials. Artists can use clay, wood, metal, leather, wool, stones, and textiles. People often use what is available in their areas. For example, people make pottery in regions where there is a lot of clay. They might make blankets if there is a lot of wool in their region. So, the type of folk art depends on where it comes from.

Pottery, saddles, rugs, and wall décor can be folk art. Folk art also includes brightly painted figurines called *alebrijes* (ah-leh-BREE-hehs). Alebrijes are imaginary creatures that combine different animal parts. For example, a figurine could have a dragon tail, cat eyes, and wolf ears. They can be made from papier-mâché or wood.

Folk art dates back to pre-Columbian time, but artists are still creating it. Many people like to collect traditional Mexican folk art because it reflects Mexican traditions and connects them to these traditions. Some people collect folk art from places they have visited on trips.

an alebrije of a flying unicorn

A woman weaves threads of different colors and textures into a patterned rug.

Mrs. Mendoza's gallery just received several new alebrijes from artists. She carefully measures them to make sure they'll fit on the display. Use the line plot to answer the questions.

Alebrijes

Height (inches)

1. How many alebrijes did Mrs. Mendoza measure?

2. How many alebrijes are less than $7\frac{1}{2}$ inches?

3. If all of the alebrijes measuring $7\frac{4}{8}$ inches are stacked on top of one another, how tall will they be?

23

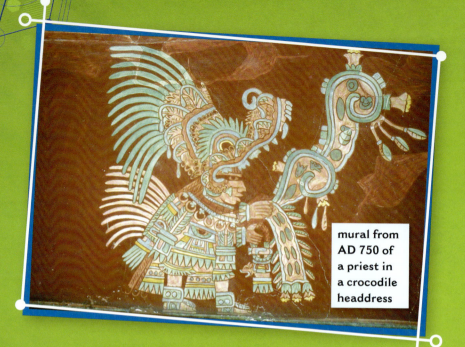

mural from AD 750 of a priest in a crocodile headdress

Murals

Murals are large paintings that are painted on dry walls or on wet **plaster**. The paint dries into the plaster, making the design permanent. This type of mural is called a fresco.

Murals in Mexico date back about 2,500 years. The Olmecs were the first people to paint murals there. They painted on the walls of caves. The paintings show their people and leaders. These paintings have faded over the years. But, efforts are being made to protect what is left of them.

The **custom** of painting murals didn't end. Many murals were painted after the Mexican Revolution. The war began in 1910. It ended in 1920. After many years of battles, the government asked artists to paint murals. They wanted to unite people and celebrate their culture. The large murals showed the nation's people. They showed the history of the country, too. Many people were not able to read. But, people did not have to read to understand the nation's history. They could look at the paintings instead. Fortunately, some of these murals still exist!

This mural painted from 1929–1945 by Diego Rivera shows Mexico's history.

TIERRA Y LIBERTAD

Traditions Today

History can be told through written stories. It can also be told orally through stories that are passed along. Artifacts can tell about history, too. They can help us learn about people who lived in the past.

In Mexico, many people still have the same values as their ancestors. Family and community are still central parts of life. Families still spend time together making meals. They use metates and molcajetes to make meals the way they were made in the past.

People also still make homemade folk art. It is sold in markets in Mexico. People buy ornaments, such as ceramic figures and jewelry.

Artifacts show that values and traditions have been carried on from the past. These artifacts give information about what was important to people back then. They help people understand the past, so they can shape the future.

A woman teaches her granddaughter to make tortillas.

handcrafted
Mexican folk art

Problem Solving

A gallery wants to feature sculptures based on the works of the Toltecs and Olmecs. The gallery is asking artists to create replicas of the original statues. Imagine that you are one of those artists. Answer the questions to find out more about the original statues and the replicas that you are creating.

1. The Toltec warrior statues at Tula are each about 460 centimeters tall. How many millimeters is this?

2. The replica of the Toltec warrior statue will be one-fifth as tall. What is the height of the replica in centimeters and millimeters? Is the height of the replica greater than or less than 1 meter? How do you know?

3. The site at Tula has 4 warrior statues. So, the gallery wants to have 4 replicas. If the replicas lie end-to-end during shipment, how much space is needed in centimeters and millimeters?

4. One of the Olmec head sculptures has a mass of about 7,250 kilograms. What is its mass in grams?

5. The replica of the Olmec head sculpture will be made of a lighter material than basalt. It will only have one-fiftieth of the mass of the original. What is the mass of the replica in kilograms and grams?

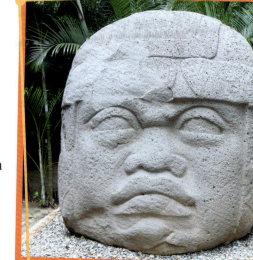

6. The replica of the Olmec head sculpture will be 3 meters tall, which is the same height as the original. What is the height of the replica in centimeters and millimeters?

Glossary

ancestors—family members from the past

artifacts—objects made by humans in the past that usually have cultural or historical meaning

basalt—a type of black rock that comes from volcanoes

ceramic—made from baked clay and heated at varying temperatures

culture—beliefs and customs of a group of people

custom—a tradition of people in a particular group or place

glazes—liquid mixtures that become shiny and smooth when dried

gourds—types of fruit with hard shells

imprinted—marked by pressing against a surface

kilns—ovens used for heating, drying, or baking pottery

murals—large paintings

ornaments—small, fancy objects that are used to decorate other things

plaster—a wet substance that hardens when it dries and is used to smooth walls

potter's wheels—machines with disks that artists place wet clay on to shape it into pottery

pottery—clay objects made by hand and baked at a high temperature

pre-Columbian—a person, time, or culture before Christopher Columbus arrived in the Americas in 1492

sculptures—art pieces made by carving or molding clay, stone, or metal

tradition—a story, belief, art, or custom passed down to younger people

values—strong beliefs about what is important or acceptable

vessels—containers used for holding or storing items

Index

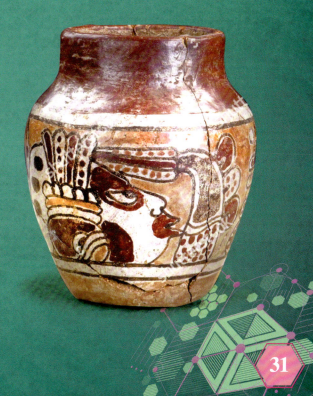

Answer Key

Let's Explore Math

page 9:

Small: 10 in., 8 in.; Medium: $1\frac{1}{2}$ ft., 1 ft.; Large: 1 ft., 10 in., $16\frac{1}{2}$ in. The metates are longer than they are wide, because each length measurement is greater than the width measurement.

page 11:

1. 86 hrs.
2. 5,160 min.
3. Almost 4 full days, because 86 hrs. is 3 days, 14 hrs.

page 13:

Javier drinks more than 1 L of water; 3×350 is 1,050 mL, and there are 1,000 mL in 1 L.

page 15:

1. 72 in.
2. 12 in., or 1 ft.

page 17:

Drum A: 18 in.; Drum B: 24 in.; Drum C: 30 in.; Drum D: 36 in.; Drum E: 42 in.; Patterns may include that the lengths increase by 6 in. each time because 6 in. = $\frac{1}{2}$ ft.

page 19:

Tres Zapotes, Monument A: 1,470 mm; San Lorenzo, Head 10: 1,800 mm; La Venta, Monument 3: 198 cm; San Lorenzo, Head 7: 270 cm; Rancho La Cobata, Monument 1: 3,400 mm

page 23:

1. 10
2. 4
3. $22\frac{4}{8}$ in., $22\frac{1}{2}$ in., or 1 ft. and $10\frac{1}{2}$ in.

Problem Solving

1. 4,600 mm
2. 92 cm; 920 mm; Less than 1 m. Explanations will vary, but may include that 1 m is 100 cm, or 1,000 mm, and the replica is only 92 cm, or 920 mm, tall.
3. 368 cm; 3,680 mm
4. 7,250,000 g
5. 145 kg; 145,000 g
6. 300 cm; 3,000 mm